CHRISTIAN SOLDIER

Write On Sister

authorHOUSE®

AuthorHouse™ UK
1663 Liberty Drive
Bloomington, IN 47403 USA
www.authorhouse.co.uk
Phone: 0800.197.4150

Published by AuthorHouse 08/08/2017

ISBN: 978-1-5246-6825-9 (sc)
ISBN: 978-1-5246-6824-2 (e)

Print information available on the last page.

This book is printed on acid-free paper.

To all persecuted Christians,
Who are not afraid to speak up against injustice
And to those who would like to have a deeper relationship with God

Proverbs 3:5-6 (NKJV)
Trust in the Lord with all your heart,
And lean not on your own understanding;
In all your ways acknowledge Him,
And He shall direct your paths.

CONTENTS

Acknowledgements

As always first and foremost I would like to thank my Heavenly Father, The Almighty God, for His strength and amazing saving grace. I have a great relationship with God, through Jesus and He continues to amaze me every day. Without God's help I am able to do nothing, so I thank him for helping me to write and publish this book. Writing this book was a big challenge however I am grateful that God gave me the ability to keep on persevering. God helped me to believe in myself and gave me more determination. There were days when I felt like given up on my book project; though after consultation with God I kept on going. God was there to guide and direct me all the way. I would often pray and have conversations with Jesus, and the Holy Spirit encouraged me and let me know that I was doing the right thing by publishing this book. Whilst writing this book, my faith in God grew stronger and I was able to develop my spiritual life in a positive way. I also thank Jesus for being my one true friend.

I appreciate the work that the famous civil rights leader, Martin Luther King Jr did in the past. He was a strong, powerful, black Christian man whose passion regarding what he believed in helped to create positive change. Reading books about Martin Luther King JR has had a positive influence on my life. I appreciate the fact that he strongly advocated non-violence as the way forward to dealing with racism and discrimination.

Kwame Nkrumah, who was the first president of Ghana, is a man whom I also admire. He led Ghana to independence from Britain on March 6th 1957.

I would like to thank all the great artists and musicians whose music has encouraged me throughout my life. Some of which include Christian artists such as, Kathryn Scott, Fred Hammond, Kirk Franklin, Sounds of Blackness, The Winnans, Truce, Nu Colours, Alvin Slaughter, J Moss and Donnie Mclurkin, to name but a few. I have also enjoyed listening to music by S Club 7, Nine Yards, Aretha Franklin and Earth Wind and Fire. Music has always inspired me ever since I was a child up until now.

A big thank you goes out to the Bill Gidda, the photographer who took the photographs that, I used for this book from Eye Media Studios in London.

A big thank you goes out once again to my publishers, Author House. I realise that I would not have any of my books published if it were not for them. I love and respect them very much and I hope to publish many more books with them in future. Their encouragement and support has helped me a great deal. I realise that there are people in my life who are willing to help me to develop my talents and skills.

I would also like to thank everyone who brought a copy of my first book, 'Free with Words'. The feeling was great when somebody showed interest in wanting to read my book and I hope they enjoyed it. Hopefully people will enjoy this book too.

Introduction

'Write on Sister' is a book containing four different chapters consisting of real life events that I have personally experienced. I started writing this book in 2015 whilst being a patient at a psychiatric hospital in London. That was something good that happened while I was there. I decided to write this book because when I wrote and published my first book, 'Free with Words', it was such an exciting, challenging and amazing experience, that it was inevitable that I would eventually write another book. I did not realise that I would write another book so soon. The inspiration for writing this book came about through the many different experiences that I have had in my life, both good and bad. I realised that I had a lot to write about and decided to break the book into four different chapters. At the end of the book, there is a selection of poems. I have seen some autobiographies in book shops and libraries and they tend to be large books with many pages, usually hardback. This book does not contain many pages and I tried to go for quality rather than quantity.

It is my intention that 'Write on Sister' will appeal to various different people. This book is very different to my first book. Although this book does contain some poems, ultimately this book is an autobiographical book about some of the things that I have experienced throughout my life. The poems included in this book are also based on real life events.

I do not claim to be perfect and neither do I claim to know everything. Something very important that I do know is that Jesus Christ loves us so much that He died for me and you. This may be the first time that you are hearing about Jesus Christ, or you may have already heard about Him. Jesus Christ was said to be the Son of God, the Great Messiah, Saviour, Light of the world and many other things. Before you continue reading this book, I would like to suggest that you take time to pray. If you do not know how to pray, then you can start communicating with God, by talking to Him in your own way. I have never seen God before, but I talk to Him every day. Praying may seem strange to you at first if you are not used to doing it, but keep at it and it gets easier. The more God sees your hunger, desire and willingness to communicate with Him, then He will give you the ability to make your prayer life better.

Another thing that I would like to say about this book is that it is not my intention to offend anyone in anyway, by what I have written. It is quite the contrary, in the sense that I actually want to inspire my readers. I have come to realise that life can be an extraordinary journey for all of us. Life is not always easy and can be very difficult at times, but it is a learning process. I have heard a saying that says 'Sometimes you have to learn the hard way.' I believe that it is possible to learn something new every day. This could be about ourselves, about others or something. Whilst I was in the process of writing this book, I learnt a lot about myself. I also discovered what God is capable of doing in our lives if we place our trust in Him. Dear readers, I would strongly urge you to take the opportunity to have faith in Jesus Christ, He is someone who will never let you down.

School photograph taken at age 9

School photograph taken at age 11.

Chapter 1

The Making Of A Christian Woman

THE MAKING OF A CHRISTIAN WOMAN

I had a pleasant childhood, I remember playing and laughing a lot. Primary school was great and I excelled at learning and developing my writing skills. It was while I was a pupil at primary school, where a great foundation was prepared for me and I first learnt about Jesus Christ. In morning assembly, we would regularly say the Lord's Prayer and sing Christian hymns. I always felt different to others even as a child. I was not a shy individual, though at the same time, I was not too talkative and I enjoyed being quiet. When I was at home, my dad would often say loudly to me, 'Speak up, speak up.' He was quite loud and I think that he wanted me to be like him. Though I am very grateful, because of my father I am now more confident and not afraid to speak up, even in difficult situations. I loved the primary school that I went to in Islington, North London. I had lots of friends and good teachers. One of my teachers in particular was a great inspiration to me. It was always a pleasure to go to school every day, just so that I could see him. He taught me and the other students many things including English, athletics, gymnastics and hand writing skills. I felt my teacher was so cool, he even taught us how to sing songs by the Beatles. Because of my teacher, I developed in certain areas. I was the fastest runner in my primary school out of all the girls, and I could also run faster than some of the boys. I had very good handwriting when I was at school, one of the best in the class. Samples of my writing were often placed on the classroom wall. I also showed some artistic ability. My teacher showed that he cared about his student's and he wanted us to do well. I was a very creative child and my special favourite teacher managed to bring out my childhood talents to the surface. I have never met a man like him and I am glad that I had such a positive person in my life that was willing to go out of his way to help me grow and develop.

Reading was something that I was encouraged to do when I was very young. I used to love reading books such as, Milly Molly Mandy by Joyce Lankester Brisley, My Naughty Little Sister by Dorothy Edwards and also Topsy and Tim by Jean Adamson and Gareth Adamson. I used to look forward to going to the library every week, so that I could find a good book to read. I also enjoyed reading comics which I used to buy every week with my pocket money. I enjoyed the interesting stories about girls and I liked the pictures. At primary school, we were taught and encouraged to do joined up hand writing with fountain pens and ink. I enjoyed doing this very much. I always used to find that the six week's summer holidays when schools close was quite difficult. I think that I used to get bored and I used to miss school. A couple of years before I left primary school, I was allowed to go into the school in the summer holidays, to help the teachers prepare for the new term with one of my best friends. I enjoyed doing this. Christmas was always a special time of year for me at primary school. One year we put on a performance of the nativity play and I had the privilege of playing the important part of the Virgin Mary. I was very happy that I was chosen out of all of my friends to have such an important part in the play. I also enjoyed music while at school and can remember my music teacher. I was in the school choir and also learnt how to play the recorder and the guitar. I can remember that we often used to have after school disco's every week. We were encouraged to bring any music that we had at home to the disco. I would sometimes take one of my sister's records by a group called the Whispers. I liked the songs 'It's a love thing' and also 'And the beat goes on'. Looking back now, I am surprised that I was listening to such groovy music at such a young age, though maybe it is because I am blessed with natural rhythm and appreciate good music. I can remember going on a school trip to Devon for a week which I enjoyed. We stayed on a farm and would regularly see animal's every day. This holiday was a great experience for me, it was the first time that I had travelled out of London and been away from my family. Everything seemed different, even the smells in the air. It was so nice to be surrounded by nature and greenery instead of being stuck in the city of London.

I used to love playing with my Cindy doll when I was a child, that my mother bought me as a present for Christmas one year. I managed to build up a collection of clothes for her. I particularly liked her long blonde hair which I would regularly comb. I eventually learnt how to braid hair on my Cindy doll. There was an Asian family who used to live next door to my family including two young boys. One of the boys was in my class at school. I would usually go to their house almost every day to play with them; we used to enjoy playing with Lego together. I often wonder what that family is doing now and would like to see them again. I sometimes see some of my old school friends, though not often. Most of the ones I see tend to now have children of their own.

When I was at primary school, I did once have a difficult experience. It was there that I first experienced somebody making up a lie about me and discovered early on the damage that lies can cause. One of my sisters was in the same school as me at one time. I was in the infants and she was in a higher class. At lunch time the infants would play on one side of the playground and the older children would play on the other side. I was very shocked and upset when one afternoon, one of my teachers approached me in the playground and said that I had gone and told my sister to hit one of my friends. I had never told my sister any such thing. Now that I am older, many people continue to make up lies and false accusations about me and I remember that this started at school. Although it has to be said that I am so glad that I went to the primary school that I went to. I often wish that I could turn the clock back and be a child again, so that I could go back to the same school. If there is one person I would like to see again, then it would be my old favourite teacher. I would love to know how he is and also thank him for helping me to be the special woman that I am today.

When I was a child, I always felt that there was someone great looking out for me. I felt safe most of the time. I used to hear an inner voice when I was growing up which I still sometimes hear as an adult. Now that I am a Christian and older, I believe that the inner voice that I often hear is the voice of God. The voice I used to hear when I was younger used to tell me not to worry and that because of what I would go through, that I would one day be a very special person.

I can remember the first time that a white child made a negative comment about the colour of my black skin. One year in the six weeks holiday I was allowed to go to a summer school where I did lots of different activities along with other children. This kept me busy while school was closed and I quite enjoyed it. It was approaching the pearly festival and I was asked to be a pearly princess. The pearly tradition began in 1875 by a young boy called Henry Croft. Henry was born in an orphanage, though had to leave at the age of thirteen. Henry's first job was as a road sweeper in a market. He got to know the market traders and made many friends. The market traders wore buttons which were sewn on their clothes. Henry liked their way of life and the market traders were very caring. Eventually Henry decided that he would like to make a positive difference by helping others including children back at his old orphanage. He started collecting buttons that had fallen off of people clothes. When he had enough buttons, he then began to sew them on his own clothes. As he got older he did charity work. The pearly tradition still continues today. I enjoyed preparing my clothes for a couple of days by sticking lots of buttons on them. On the day of the pearly festival, I enjoyed it very much though I was very saddened when we were returning back to the centre by coach. A boy who was about my age was very rude to me about my colour. I was very upset and almost cried. One of the adult assistants told him off. I now realise that this was the first time that I experienced racism. Before this difficult incident, my colour had never been an issue for me or anybody else, I always felt excepted by everybody and most of my friends were white. I was really made to feel different on this occasion and I felt like I did not belong, which was upsetting because I was so young and had never experienced that treatment before.

The transition from primary school to secondary school seemed like quite a big one. Primary school to me seemed like one big game where I was always playing. When I went to secondary school, I was made to do lots of studying. We were given lots of homework to do and more responsibility. I had quite a fun time at secondary school, though I wish I had studied much harder and taken things more seriously. I enjoyed playing netball and always played the position of centre which

I thought was great. I liked the fact that I had the opportunity to start off the game by having the ball first, then passing it to my friends. It was while I was at secondary school that I went on a trip to France which I enjoyed. I was becoming more interested in fashion at this stage. At times I felt that some of my friends wore more fashionable clothes than me. Though I was always well dressed and appreciated the fact that I used to get weekly pocket money, to buy some of my own things. I was always satisfied with the clothes that I had as a child and I was taught the importance of valuing money and spending wisely.

At about the age of 14 while at secondary school was when I first heard music by the American singer Michael McDonald. I heard his song that he sings with James Ingram being played on the radio. The song is called 'Ya Mo Be There', and I still enjoy listening to it now as an adult. I bought one of his cassette tapes and listened to it nearly every day. I think that Michael McDonald has one of the most amazing voices. My favourite song is another song sang by Michael McDonald and Darwin Hobbs called 'Everyday'. That song always gets me up on the floor and dancing. I used to like watching Top of the Pops when I was young. Top of the Pops was a weekly show on television showing the latest singers. Other programmes which I used to enjoy watching at home were Little House on the Prairie, and the Walton's. I used to find watching Laurel and Hardy highly entertaining and I still love their comedy. I remember one year on Christmas Eve, I first saw the film singing in the Rain starring Gene Kelly, from that day on I began to enjoy watching American musicals. I always enjoyed Christmas as a child, all the sparkly tinsel, presents and nice food was great. I first saw the film Pollyanna starring Haley Mills when I was at school. This is a film I still enjoy watching even as an adult. I think that Haley Mills is a great actress and it is a pleasure to watch her films.

I now find it strange that in careers lessons when I was at secondary school I was never told about the opportunity of going to university in future. However, I had made up my mind quite early on that I wanted to become a chef. Just before I completed secondary school, I went on a work placement for one week at a restaurant in London which I enjoyed. After I completed the work placement, I knew that I was making the right decision in wanting to go to catering college. Just after I left secondary school at age sixteen, I was very excited about being offered a place as a student at one of the top catering colleges in the country. I had applied for a place on a three year professional chefs Diploma course while at secondary school. Home Economics was my favourite subject. I enjoyed making cakes and taking them home to share with my family. I also enjoyed studying English at school. I remember reading books such as 'Jane Eyre' by Charlotte Bronte which I really enjoyed. I was disappointed regarding not being chosen by my English teacher who was also my tutor, to do O Level English. I was studying for CSE'S, while some of my classmates where studying for O Levels. When I left school I achieved a grade 1 CSE in English, which was apparently equivalent to an O Level. I received a lower grade in Home Economics and was so disappointed that I never even went back to the school to collect my certificate. At the age of sixteen when I was in my final year of secondary school, I became an aunty for the first time, I was so happy. I now currently have five nieces and three nephews. It has been a real pleasure to watch them grow up over the years and develop and I love them all very much.

Cooking was one of the things that I loved to do most. I was inspired to cook and go to catering college by watching my mother cook when I was a child. My mother still continues to be the best cook that I know and I am grateful for her delicious food. I also used to like watching Delia Smith's Cookery Course programme on television every week. I was fascinated about how people could take raw ingredients and turn it into something different that also looked and tasted nice. On the day of my interview for a place at Catering College, I had a tour of the college with my mother who came with me The whole experience of being there was very exciting. When I was finally offered a place after my interview, it felt like the best thing that had ever happened to me. I had never experienced so much joy before. Catering college lasted for three years and I loved it, I made lots of friends there and my confidence developed.

After I left catering college, I had various jobs including working for a television company, a theatre, and a residential home for the elderly. I also worked in a hospital for five years and in a prison as a chef for a couple of months. I never felt truly happy in places where I worked, usually because I did not get on with management and often disagreed with some of the practices that were going on in the work place. By this time, I had become quite an outspoken person and if I saw something that I did not agree with, I was not afraid to speak up. Though when I did speak up in most of the places where I worked, the management did not seem to like it. I feel that the best job that I had was when I worked in a local women's prison. This was both exciting and challenging. I only stayed there for a couple of months but in that time I learnt a lot about myself and other people. I have a desire to work in a prison again one day, though in a chaplaincy department. In the past I wanted to be a prison officer, now I would much prefer to help set people free by helping to lead them to Christ through evangelism, rather than keeping people locked up. I find it quite fascinating that although I found it to be very difficult working in a prison, I would still like to work in one again.

At the age of 24, I was very happy when I was offered a flat by my local council which I accepted. I was so happy to finally have my own flat and more independence. I can recall that when I was in my twenties, I had an accident when I was hit by an oncoming car on a road in Islington, London. I do not think that I was looking properly when I crossed the road. The car did not stop and I simply carried on walking and went to do my shopping. I was slightly startled, though not hurt. I did not tell anybody about what happened until years later. I was also hit by a bicycle on a London street when I was in my twenties. In the year 2000 I began an advanced course in Health and Social Care at a college in London. It was my intention to complete the two - year part-time course, and then go to university to study social work. I wanted to become a social worker and specialise in mental health, but I was unable to complete the course and I became ill. It was while studying at this College that I had my first suicidal thought. I remember that I almost took an overdose one evening. My experience at the college was very strange and difficult. I enjoyed some aspects of the course, though began to realise that most of the staff and students where targeting me and treating me unfairly. Whilst at the college, I was physically attacked by a student while playing basketball. I ended up having to go to hospital with a sprained ankle and I was on crutches for a couple of weeks. I learnt about psychology and sociology, though the main thing I learnt while I was at this college was how people could be so cruel to a person, unfortunately that person was me. It was while I was at College that I learnt how to write and compile reports. I have since gone on to write many reports of my own. I was unable to complete the course and left the college feeling disheartened.

In the year 2000, something amazing happened to me, when at the age of 29; I became a Born-again Christian by giving my life to Jesus Christ. It was the best decision that I have ever made. Around the same time, I was having to deal with a lot of difficult challenges in my life, including family problems. In the year 2000, I also ended up as a patient in a psychiatric hospital and was sectioned for the first time under the Mental Health Act. I must point out that I have never felt that Jesus or the fact that I became a Christian was the cause of me becoming ill. I became saved; a term which some Christians use to describe what Jesus does to them. Jesus is also known as a Saviour who saves individuals from the consequences of sin, which leads to death, by transforming their lives for the better. I began to realise that Jesus Christ was the solution to the difficulties that I was experiencing and began to develop my faith in Him. After I became a Christian, my faith was constantly being tested. I noticed that many people began to change towards me. The few people that I had in my life who I thought were my friends suddenly changed and began to treat me differently, some of them in quite a disrespectful manner. Looking back now, I realise that when I became a Christian, many people did not like it and wanted to see my downfall. This has now become much more apparent to me because I now know what being a follower of Christ means. I feel that what I began to experience and still experience is persecution in some type of way. The Bible does say that Christians will suffer persecution, trials and tribulation, because of what we believe in. Many people do not like it when individuals choose to follow Christ, because some people choose to follow the Devil.

Around the time that I became a Christian, I discovered a poetry book by the famous author, Emily Bronte. I found the book in a bookshop in Central London. When I took the book home I was immediately drawn to Emily's extraordinary way of writing. The book encouraged me to write poetry too. Two of my favourite Emily Bronte poems are, 'Strong I Stand', and 'No Coward Soul Is Mine'. Emily Bronte is a woman whom I admire very much and I believe that God led me to that particular bookshop to buy her book. There are other women whom I admire including my mother and my three sisters. I admire the fact that the women in my family are very hard working and emotionally strong

In the year 2000, the same year that I became a Christian, I was taken to a psychiatric hospital for the first time. I had been taken there one night, after setting off a fire alarm in general hospital. Being in a psychiatric hospital for the first time left me feeling lonely and confused. It was a terrifying experience. I remember crying a lot because I was so scared and feeling very distressed. The thing that made my situation even more difficult was the fact that a young lady who was a member of staff kept on laughing at me. I was later taken to another psychiatric hospital in London, where I was then sectioned under the mental health act. It was there, where I was first treated with medication. I was not taken to any local Accident and Emergency Department to be formally assessed by a mental health team. Within the first couple of nights at the psychiatric hospital I can remember on one occasion, I had restless legs syndrome after staff had given me medication. I now believe that the restless legs were a side effect from the medication I was being forced to take. I had to keep moving my legs around the bed. One particular night, I fell out of the bed twice, banging my head badly on the bedside cabinet. I got up from the floor and walked down the hospital corridor in a daze, and in pain with a lump on my head. I told staff what happened, however they did nothing and I walked back to the room and went to bed. Well, enough for the moment about my time spent in psychiatric hospitals.

This will all be revealed in the next chapter of this book, called 'From Adversity to Victory.'

When I became a Christian, I began to write poetry, I feel that it was a gift from God. I managed to build up a collection of poems. In 2012 whilst browsing on the internet, I came across information about an American publishing company called Author House. I then began to develop the idea to write and publish a book. I left my information with Author House requesting more information. Soon after, I was contacted by a publishing consultant via the telephone. We had a great conversation and that set the ball rolling. I continued to write poetry to add to my collection. I have an older brother who is also a writer and in the past, he encouraged me to do a writing course. I enrolled on a home study poetry course with the Writers Bureau that I completed in 2014. With help and support from my tutor, I was able to learn new writing skills and techniques. My writing improved, and by 2015, my first book of poems called 'Free with Words' was published. I was so happy when I received the first copy of my book through the post. I am glad that God has blessed me with many gifts and talents.

I think that at this stage of my book, it is important to mention about me being a Christian and attending church. I have been to many churches throughout my life in London and was a member of a particular local church for many years. However due to the fact that I have had many bad and difficult experiences in churches, I no longer attend. I have had some good times in church however these days when I attend church I usually disagree with some of the things that happen there. I now do my praying and worshiping in my own house which I also call the Holy Ghost Tabernacle. I often feel sad at the fact that for some reason I have no friends, especially Christian friends. Then I think to myself I have the greatest friend, who is always with me and that is Jesus Christ. I would love to have some support from other fellow believers. I would love to have my own Christian house fellowship one day, rather than me going to other churches and not feeling welcome or feeling unhappy. I had an unfortunate experience where I was removed from the same church twice by police, when I had done nothing wrong. I actually used to love going to that particular church and I went there for many years until I realised that for some strange reason they were discriminating against me.

On another separate occasion, I was standing outside the same church and overheard two pastors saying that I was mad. I wanted to be in the church because it felt as though I had nowhere else to go. I would often go to the church everyday sometimes two or three times a day. I had no close friends in the church though I used to enjoy going to the services which I usually found quite encouraging. Then strange things began happening in the church. I would sometimes go to deliverance services which included pastors and assistants laying hands on people. Whenever they laid hands on my head and prayed, they would often say strange things, spin me round in circles like I had a demon inside of me and leave me feeling discouraged. On one occasion I was almost wrestled to the floor by a young male assistant who was trying to make it seem as though I was possessed with an evil spirit. On another occasion a male assistant laid his hands on my head and held it so hard that I was left with a headache. I think the business of laying hands on people is very serious and it should only be practiced by mature Christians who actually know what they are doing, otherwise it could lead to serious implications. On another separate occasion, I once had an accident in the same church when I banged my head badly on a staircase as I stood up from a chair. I was very surprised that I was surrounded by many people in the church and not one person asked me if I was alright. I left in pain and thinking to myself is this the way Christians are supposed to treat each other? I knew that it was not, but I can never force someone to care for me when it is obvious that they do not. Many people go to church because they are struggling in life and need help and support. They want to leave the church feeling better and not worse. I continued to go to the same church for a long time, even though I disagreed with some of their practices. Eventually I made the important decision to leave that particular church because I was concerned that if I did not, then something very bad would happen to me there. I have since tried going to other churches, though now I worship at my own house, The Holy Ghost Tabernacle.

I have noticed that these days, many Christians seem to be practising something that is quite similar to Psychology instead of Christianity. I think that there is something very seriously wrong with churches in this country. I have attended over ten different churches in London in the past, with the hope that I could find Christians who showed that they cared. I now have no intention of ever going back to any of the churches I have been to. I would much rather stay in my own church by myself with Jesus instead of going to another church that is packed with people who are not genuine.

I love worshiping and praying at the Holy Ghost Tabernacle. I love my intimate times that I spend with Jesus. I do understand that it is good to fellowship with other believers and there is sometimes strength in numbers. I think that God knows that I have had difficulties in all of the churches that I have been to, because he sees and knows everything. I also think that he knows that I struggle to make friends these days, even though I am a very friendly person. I have had to put up with a lot of harassment and discrimination throughout my life, especially recently. I am often targeted by people I know as well as people I do not know. I do realise that because I am a Christian, I should not be afraid of anyone or anything, because I have Gods Holy Spirit inside of me that gives power. Though at the same time, I have suffered a lot in my life and been hurt, sometimes physically by people. I still place my faith in Jesus Christ because I feel that He is the only one who truly helps me. At times I used to wonder why I was going through so many difficulties and I was a Christian. I used to think that because I was a Christian, then I should not be suffering. I have read parts of the Bible and it talks about how as believers we will have to suffer for what we believe in. What I find difficult to understand is when people claim to be Christians but then they treat me badly. I often think are they real Christians? Because I realise that not everyone is honest, especially in the world which we now live in. There are many people who claim to be Christians, who are not. I have to admit and say that since I became a Christian, I have still done some wrong things and I have even committed some sins. This is otherwise known as when a person back slides and reverts to previous bad behaviour. I am not perfect now, though I am much wiser than I used to be and not so naïve. I am not led so easily into temptation anymore and I am very careful whom I choose to trust in this world and who I would choose to be my friend. Many people have let me down throughout my life and I currently trust nobody in this world, apart from Jesus Christ. God continues to amaze me every day and He never disappoints me.

Since becoming a Christian, I have learnt to love myself more. I now have more confidence than I have ever had previously in my life. Although I lead a very challenging and at times difficult life, I now love being me. I would not want to be anyone else. God made me the way I am for a reason. I am different to most people I meet in fact I have never met anyone like me.

I love being a Christian woman, though it is not always easy. I often pray for God to make me be a more beautiful woman, both inside and out. A person can be very beautiful but then have a very bad character; I do not want to be like that. My looks are important to me though what is more important is how I am on the inside. I want to be a woman of virtue. I want people to see a difference in me when they meet me. I want to show love and respect to others always. I also want to have self-respect. I do not want to do anything to offend anyone, especially God.

It is a real pleasure being a Christian woman. Being a Christian is more than just an interest or hobby. It is a way of life that I am trying to develop daily. I feel that everybody's Christian walk with Jesus is different. The fact that I have no Christian friends often makes me wonder, how does my life compare to other believers? I try to seek guidance and direction from God as often as possible and also pray daily. I realise that there is plenty of room for improvement in my life. With God's help and support and my strong faith in Him and in myself, I will one day become a more beautiful, stronger and wiser woman. In the meantime, I continue to thank God for making me to be the woman that I currently am at the moment.

Chapter 2

From Adversity To Victory

FROM ADVERSITY TO VICTORY

In July 2015, two months after the publication of my first book, 'Free with Words', I suffered with another bout of depression and found myself being sectioned under the mental health act yet again in another psychiatric hospital. This was now the eighteenth time that I had been in a psychiatric hospital. In the space of twelve months, I had been moved to four different hospitals in and around London. 'From Adversity to Victory' is an insight into what goes on in some of the psychiatric hospitals in London and my ongoing struggle to stay well and out of hospital. This chapter of my book gives a graphic account into what many people do not see, or experience once a person is sectioned under the mental health act. When a person is sectioned in a psychiatric hospital, they are not allowed to leave unless a doctor says they can. I am usually placed on a Section 3 which means that doctors could keep me in hospital for up to six months. The patient can also be forced to take any medication that the doctor has prescribed, without their consent. Patients are allowed to appeal against their section by going through a mental health tribunal.

On the 17th of July 2015, I can recall going to the local office in London where my community mental health team is based. When I arrived at the office, I knew what I was going to do. I got out my mobile phone from my bag and I called the police. I told the police that I wanted to report serious crimes that the mental health team had committed against me. These crimes included physical assault, as well as making up lies and false allegations about me which amounts to slander. I felt very angry towards the mental health team, because I had been treated very unfairly by them, years. I had been wrongly diagnosed with an illness which I did not have and I was being forced to take medication in the form of tablets and depot injections in my bottom, which I felt was physical assault. The Depot is medication in the form of an injection that I had to have every three weeks in my bottom. This procedure is painful and always leaves me with lumps on my bottom and other serious side effects, such as painful lumps in my breast, weight gain, and tiredness, stiffness in muscles and in joints. One of my doctors once told me that the depot injection that she was forcing me to take could cause me to have breast cancer. This was while I was a patient at a psychiatric hospital. This information that the doctor told me about breast cancer devastated me so much, that I took an overdose while I was at the hospital. I got some tablets from my flat while I was on leave and brought it back to the hospital with me. One afternoon I felt depressed and very concerned that I would get breast cancer from the depot injection I was taking. After I took the overdose, I ended up at a local, general hospital because I was so sick with vomiting and stomach ache.

I was concerned that the mental health team had tried me on over twelve different tablets, since they had been working with me. The tablets were mainly anti-psychotics which all gave me side effects. I have never even suffered with psychotic symptoms. I told the team on many occasions that I was unhappy about the way that they were treating me. I told them that I wanted to work with a different team. I would often get sick when I was in the community, and then end up in hospital. Upon my release, I would often be told by my doctors that I would have to work with the same mental health team and that there was not another team in the community who I could work with. I knew that I needed some support in the community from health professionals, though I had never received it. The lies and false allegations that had been made up about me were very distressing. I had been accused of slapping a doctor, attacking a policeman, being outside with a bottle of whiskey, being outside naked and being rude to members of the public. All of these allegations were untrue. I could not believe that a team that was supposed to be helping me to stay well in the community were actually treating me so badly.

Eventually, it reached a stage where I felt that it was about time that I took some serious action. In November 2014 I attempted to commit suicide by trying to jump in front of an oncoming train at Camden Town Station in London. A member of the public pulled me back, just as the train was approaching and just as I was about to jump. At the time, I had become very depressed regarding the treatment that I had been receiving from mental health services in my life. Looking back now, I am very grateful to the man who stopped me from killing myself at the Station. I would like to meet him again so that I could thank him. One year later after that terrible incident, I was still being forced to work with the same team, and I was still having serious difficulties with them. I no longer wanted to work with a team that was continually discriminating against me and harassing me, which was causing me to be sick.

So on the 17th July 2015, while I was in my house I put on some smart clothes and shoes, that morning. I then made my way to the office where my mental health team was based. I had a copy of my recently published book, 'Free with Words', to give myself some added confidence. When I arrived at the office, I knew exactly what I was going to do, I took my mobile phone from my bag and I called the police, to report the crimes which had been committed against me. The police told me that they would be at the premises within the hour, after I gave them the address of where I was. I continued to wait patiently. Around forty minutes later, three members of the mental health team came to speak to me. The three team members were my psychiatric consultant, care co-ordinator and the team manager. They then proceeded to explain to me that the police had been in contact with them, and had told them that they were not coming to see me and that I should talk to the them instead. I was very disappointed that the police where not coming, though I continued to remain calm and assertive. After a short conversation with the three ladies, about why I called the police, I left the office. My psychiatric consultant had recently stopped all of my medication, at my request. However, I was still determined to fight for justice regarding the appalling things that the mental health team had done to me.

As the police did not show up at the office as they said they would, when I left I decided to go to a police station in central London. When I arrived there, I waited almost an hour and was not seen by anybody, so I eventually left. Before leaving, I left a copy of my poetry book, 'Free with Words' there, then made my way back to my house. Sadly, later that night I became very depressed and I ended up writing a suicide note on my laptop. I then printed out a copy of the note and took it to my local police station. I had become very unwell and this was my way of crying out for help. After the police read the letter, they suggested that it would be better for me to go to hospital. Although it was a difficult decision to make I agreed with the police that I needed to go to hospital, so I was driven there. I was assessed at the general hospital and then later sectioned for the eighteenth time. I was taken to a local psychiatric hospital; this was very frustrating for me, to find myself in hospital yet again. For over a month, prior to going into hospital, I had been phoning the Samaritans for some support, because I had been having suicidal thoughts. I was initially not able to talk to anyone else about my situation though found the Samaritans helpful. I actually thought that I was getting better. It was great having people to talk to, anytime of day about my difficulties.

I had been working on a lot of different projects before I became unwell. I had been decorating my flat, looking for a job, doing a writing course and trying to start up a Christian house Fellowship group. I had published my book in May 2015, and then in July 2015 I was back in hospital. Going back to hospital was very disappointing. I am someone who works hard to try to succeed in life, even though I have faced many challenges and knock backs, I still have a strong level of determination. So I was back in hospital again, this was very difficult for me because of the numerous difficult experiences I had encountered at that particular place The first negative experience that I had there was when I was placed on depot injection for the first time. I had also been restrained by male staff which was distressing. There was one incident when I had my ankles and hands held down by two different men on a bed. Another male staff member was watching. I was then injected by a female in the bottom. I could not breathe properly when this incident was happening because I could not move my head which was in the pillow. I reported the incident to the police, though they did not come and see me. On one occasion, I found another patient dead in her bedroom on the floor, at the same hospital.

When I was admitted to hospital on the 17th July 2015, I was there for four weeks. In that time, I was put back on depot injection and also given PRN injection on one particular occasion. PRN medication is medicine that nursing staff used to give me when they felt I needed calming down. The medication always has sedative in it. I protested by threatening a member of staff. I did not actually touch anyone and I do realise that what I did was wrong. The following day I was taken a more secure unit. This was an all-female hospital and was an extremely tough experience, though part of me was happy to be leaving the other hospital. I was on close observation most of the time. Even when sleeping, the bedroom door would have to be left open with a member of staff sitting outside the room watching me, sometimes men, which I found very intrusive. The toughest part of the whole experience at this Hospital was that I was restrained quite a few times and injected in my bottom. I was at the secure unit for five weeks and had a lot of physical pain inflicted upon me. I had my arm twisted inappropriately by three different male staff on three separate occasions. I wanted to call the police and report it at the time however I was not allowed to.

Also while I was at the hospital, I developed a large lump in my left breast, I feel that this was due to the fact that I was put back on the depot injection and that I was having side effects. I made a lot of progress while I was at the hospital, even though I was very disappointed with the treatment that I was receiving there. I was due to have a hospital tribunal in August 2015, and compiled my own detailed report. On the day of the tribunal, I was taken to the meeting room then informed that the tribunal would not go ahead because my care co-ordinator from my mental health team would not be attending. This was disappointing for me especially as I thought that I had a strong case to win the tribunal. Eventually after five weeks, in a ward round meeting I was told that I would be going back to a hospital in my local borough. This caused me to have great concerns, considering everything that I experienced there in the past, including physical assault by staff. Later that day, I was told to pack my belongings. I was surprised when I was told that my diary and a beautiful handbag that I gave to staff was not amongst my possessions that I got back. The hospital had stolen my property as well as everything else that they had done to me. I still had a big lump in my breast that had not been checked by a specialist. I developed involuntary movements and would often stumble and almost fall to the ground. I also developed a tingling sensation in the sole of my left foot when I would sit down. Also I had stiffness in joints and muscles. I believed that these were all side -effects from all the injections that I was being forced to take.

Initially being at this new hospital was a pleasant relief. It was nice to be on a ward that was so calm and relaxed, with no tension and no noise. However, something was bothering me. I knew that my next depot injection was due soon, what was I going to do this time? Well I told staff about my concerns regarding depot injection. I also told them that if they inflicted physical pain on me in the form of an injection in my bottom, then I would protest by attacking a member of staff. Less than two weeks later, I was eventually given a depot injection against my will and I was so disappointed that out of my frustration and anger, I threatened to attack a member of the staff. At the time I felt that what I was doing was self- defence. Immediately after the incident, I told staff that I wanted to go to a more secure unit. I felt very let down by the Hospital. I thought that it would be the place where they would stop giving me depot injections because the ward manager initially seemed very helpful until he made up a lie about me. After that, I was eager to leave. I was honest enough to admit that I was a risk to others now, not just myself and I felt I needed to go to a different hospital.

I soon realised what people mean regarding the saying, 'Be careful what you ask for' Because I was later sent to a fourth hospital this was an awful experience. Before I left the previous Hospital, I did something that I am ashamed of. A female member of staff was coming out of the office and I pushed my way in and grabbed hold of her face. Obviously she was not happy, though at the time, I felt great. I did not apologize to her when I left that night, even though she was standing right by my side. It later dawned on me that the member of staff that I attacked before I left had been the nicest member of staff while I was there. My frustration and anger was so strong at the time that I think I attacked her because she was so nice to me, as strange as it sounds. I became annoyed with her because I felt that she was part of a brutal system that was being very unkind to me. I became disappointed that she was not helping me.

I left the Hospital at 3am in the morning, I was not told where I was going, only to another hospital. Sometime later I arrived at a private patients Hospital. Usually whenever I go to hospital, when I am given a bedroom I always make sure that I say a strong prayer when I get in there. This is because I never have any way of knowing who stayed in that room before me and what happened there. When I arrived at the new hospital, I was very tired and I completely forgot to pray when I was given my bedroom. I tried to sleep in the bed and I felt so sick that I almost vomited. I could almost sense that there were negative vibes in the room and began to wonder who had slept in the bed prior to me sleeping in it. Eventually I did go to sleep.

This new hospital was something else. It was on an all-female ward, though there were male staff working there. It became apparent very quickly that some of the women were very rude and aggressive. Especially after being there for less than two weeks, I was attacked by another patient, who was also racist towards me. I was pushed on my upper body and I stumbled backwards and almost lost my balance. When I arrived at the hospital I already had some pain in my left knee and also a large lump in my left breast which was very painful. After I was attacked, the pain in my knee and my breast became worse. I decided to call the police after I was attacked and two officers came to see me the following day. The police told me that they would work with the hospital to sort things out, though nothing was done about it. While I was a patient at the hospital, I was injected in my bottom over forty times. Within five weeks the hospital injected me fourteen times. Some of these injections were depot injections, which I would have every four weeks. The majority of the injections were PRN injections. Most of the time the staff would offer me tablets first, though I would usually refuse because I felt that I did not need their medication.

On one particular occasion, I was admittedly speaking loudly one evening. I was expressing my anger regarding being injected so many times. This was the only way that I felt that I could protest at the time. Suddenly I was approached by three male members of staff. I was told by one of the men that I was hallucinating and hearing voices, though I was actually not. I was then taken to a de-escalation room where a female member of staff injected me in the bottom. From this moment on I lost complete trust in all the staff at the hospital. On another separate occasion, I was given an injection and the following day I could not walk or talk properly because I was so heavily sedated. I feel that the procedure of physically restraining somebody when they refuse to take medication, then forcing them to take it is degrading and painful. I think that it is a very dangerous procedure to be used on anybody, especially vulnerable women. Most of the time when I have been restrained, I have not been physically harmful to anybody, but this has sometimes led to me becoming angry and aggressive. The medication always makes me feel sedated and I find it difficult to understand and agree with such a barbaric practice. Even though I have been going through this same treatment for over ten years, I will never make it easy for somebody to inject me in the bottom. Though it is very difficult for me, because when I refuse depot injection or the tablets which I am offered, I am usually held down, restrained and forced to take it, I often had my pants pulled down by men and was injected. This also happened to me at other hospitals too.

One evening, while I was a patient in a hospital I was restrained by an overweight, sweaty, male member of staff on the ward corridor, who ended up sitting, straddled on top of me before he gave me an injection in my bottom. At the same time, on that occasion a violent film was being shown in the lounge area close by, with a patient watching. The film depicted a mother and daughter being beaten and raped. I was disgusted and sickened about this whole ordeal. I still often have painful memories about the whole incident. Inappropriate programmes were often shown on the televisions in all the hospitals I have been too, with staff usually watching the programmes too. I was often left feeling shocked about the way I was being treated at these hospitals, especially by women.

On the 5th November 2015, I had a tribunal at a hospital. I prepared myself well by compiling my own report. I did not have a solicitor at the time, though found it quite strange when a solicitor came to see me on the day, saying he would represent me. I think that I had seen him somewhere in the past, but cannot quite remember where. The solicitor told me that he had been assigned to me by the hospital and the Tribunal Panel. I decided to go ahead and let him represent me which I now feel was a big mistake because he did not do anything to help me anyway. I did not see a second opinion doctor before the tribunal and my care co-ordinator was not present though the tribunal still went ahead. Another member of staff from the community mental health team did attend. As per usual, many lies were told about me in the tribunal by hospital staff, which is always very difficult for me to sit and listen too. It came as a shock to me when my doctor informed the panel that he had increased the dose of my depot injection, without personally informing me. After the tribunal, we were all told to leave the room for the panel to decide what the outcome would be. After about five minutes we were all called back to the room where I was told that I would still have to remain at the Hospital. I was unhappy, I wanted to leave. The thought of having to stay at that hospital for another day made me feel sick.

On the 23rd November 2015, I was given a copy of my treatment plan to look at which stated that I was deluded because I had been saying that I think Jesus will save me. This made me feel angry and frustrated, but I now realise this was the hospitals plan all along. They wanted to push, provoke and anger me so much that I would react back and unfortunately I did. While I was at hospital, I developed terrible pains in my gluteal muscle and my hamstring muscle as a result of being tortured so much. At one point I had to take painkillers four times a day every day for over a month because I had developed Sciatica. The anger and distress was building up inside of me every day. There were some days when I was in a lot of pain, but I did not want to ask for painkillers because female nursing staff often wore nail varnish which was unprofessional. Within the first week of being in hospital, a female member of staff made a rude comment about a lump that I had in my breast and asked me if I get paranoid because of it. I was very upset and reported her to the ward manager, though nothing was done about the situation. To be called paranoid by health professionals when I am not, is very offensive. I can recall the first time that I was called paranoid by a doctor, this was because I told her that the tablets that I was being given tasted very bitter and she turned to me and said, 'Oh you're paranoid'. Since then doctors and other so called health professionals seem to target me with this label frequently.

There was a multi-faith room at the hospital which I would sometimes go to and a computer room. It was always a pleasant relief to get time off of the ward and do something different. I often spent time in bedroom praying, worshiping and writing; I did not have my own Bible at the time until I was allowed a home visit to my flat to get one. On the 24th November 2016, I was told by my doctor at the hospital that I could have a home visit. When I eventually did have the home visit, it went well apart from the member of staff who was escorting me picked up a bottle of alcohol in Sainsbury's. I did not drink alcohol at the time and I told her that I did not want her to bring that to my house, so she went to put it back. I felt that I would not have been allowed to buy alcohol at that time, so it was therefore irresponsible for her to attempt to buy it for herself while she was escorting me on leave. I felt that what the member of staff did spoiled the whole of my home visit and I went back to the hospital feeling angry.

Loneliness was something that I did not suffer much from when I was in hospital. This was because I was always around people 24 hours a day. I actually spent most of the time in the bedroom while at hospital, though it was reassuring to know that if I needed to talk to somebody, there was always someone around. It eventually did get to a stage when I started to find it difficult to talk to the staff at the hospital, because of the negative treatment that I was being subjected to there. Something that I appreciate when I go to hospital is that I am able to have a bedroom to myself. This is very helpful and it enables me to have some privacy and do what I need to do in my own space.

By the 6th December 2015, I was thinking a lot about the fact that Christmas was approaching and I was still in hospital. I wanted to spend Christmas in my flat. I wanted to spend it on my own. Though at the same time, I did not want to feel lonely. Ideally I wanted to spend Christmas every year with someone, though I had no friends. I usually find family gatherings difficult and preferred not to be with them. On Christmas, in 2014 I was in another psychiatric hospital and it was the worst Christmas I ever had. I cried on Christmas day and staff restrained me and injected me on Boxing day. I was there for two months and it was a tough experience. I was restrained and given many injections, so I was very relieved when I left in January 2015. Four months after leaving this particular hospital, I published my first book, 'Free with Words'. This was a very big achievement for me, considering what I had been through a couple of months before.

I realise that as I am becoming older, I have become a very outspoken person and many people do not like it. This is partly because I am a black, intelligent, articulate Christian woman. Being a Christian, I am aware that in the Bible, it says that we should do all things without complaining or disputing. I am still trying to find out exactly what the scripture means and seeking Gods guidance about the best way to handle difficult situations and injustice. I feel that it is good when people speak out against injustice because this usually helps to bring about positive change. The famous civil rights leader, Martin Luther King Jr, whom I admire once said, 'The thing that we need in the world today is a group of men and women who will stand up for right and be opposed to wrong, wherever it is.' (King, 2000, p12). In the Bible, in the book of Matthew chapter 4, there are examples of where Jesus Christ stood up against the Devil. When Jesus was in the wilderness, He was tempted by the Devil. On three separate occasions, Jesus responded to the Devil by saying 'It is written'- Matthew 4:4,7,10. Jesus was able to stand up for Himself and put the Devil in His place by using the word of God.

On the 8th December 2015 I had a ward round meeting and I requested to see a second opinion doctor. I was told by my consultant that I had already seen one, which was incorrect. I realise that it had now been five months since I last went out by myself. This was difficult for me, when I am in the community I go out by myself every day. Also I was very saddened when I had a blood test and I was told by my primary nurse that the results showed that I was getting pains in my body because of the menopause. I had not even started the menopause and felt that the hospital did not want to take any responsibility for the pain they were inflicting upon me. The next time that I had a ward round meeting on the 15th December 2015 my doctor told me that I talk too much and told me that he would be increasing the dose of the depot injection. I was very angry. I always find it difficult to understand that some of the staff in these psychiatric hospitals claim to be Christians and some of them treat me in a negative way or do not speak out when their colleagues do wrong things to me. Being the type of person that I am, I could never work in a place where someone was allowed to be tortured or serious crimes were being committed against them. I have actually left a job in the past because a woman was being bullied by another work mate. I spoke to management about this on numerous occasions but they did nothing. Eventually the woman who was being bullied approached me one day and asked me why I did nothing to help her. I explained to her that I had tried, though not long after, I left the job. I made the silly mistake of going back to work there, though things were worse than before.

One morning whilst being in hospital, a second opinion doctor came to see me from the Care Quality Commission. I was very upset when she informed me that my doctor in the hospital said that I needed to take mood stabilizers, hypnotics and sleeping tablets. I was saddened that nobody in or out of the hospital were taking me seriously. While I was in hospital, my doctors changed my diagnoses from schizoid-effective disorder to schizophrenia. I was disappointed at the way these labels were being placed on me, but other than verbally express my unhappiness. I did not know what else to do. I was very happy when I was eventually given unescorted leave from hospital. It was great to be able to finally go out by myself without somebody following me and watching my every move. I was beginning to realise that over the past couple of months, I had done some things wrong and made some silly mistakes. This resulted in me having to pay the price. I wish that I had never brandished a knife at doctors or staff because it now has serious implications and will be noted down in my file.

By the time Christmas day came, I was still a patient in hospital and I was sad about it, however I tried to remain positive and tried my best to enjoy the day. It was actually quite a pleasant day. The atmosphere was nice on the ward. The staff went out of their way to make things enjoyable. I had the best Christmas lunch that I have ever had. I watched some nice programmes on television and was given a nice present by the staff. At the end of the day, I thought to myself, why was it not like that every day in hospital. I was also glad at the fact that I was not by myself and that I had some company.

I was becoming concerned that I was sleeping much more than usual which I knew was because of the increase in dose of the medication. This was very frustrating for me. When I first went to the hospital, I was always up early washed and dressed, doing my morning exercise and full of energy. Then months later after a high increase in medication, I was struggling to get up in the mornings. Sometimes I could not even get up for breakfast. I would struggle to get up in the afternoon then get washed and dressed. I was also aware that my faith was a bit low. I had actually been depressed and suicidal for months even while in hospital because I was being injected so much and was left in serious pain. I was beginning to question my faith and was wondering if I still wanted to be a Christian considering that I was suffering so much. I had no Christian friends in my life at the time and had no intention of going back to church because of negative experiences that I had previously had there.

On the 6th January 2016 my care co-ordinator from my local community mental health team came to visit me in hospital. After a brief chat, she informed me that I still needed to stay in Hospital and I would eventually go back to a hospital in my borough. I was once again left feeling very disappointed. On the 15th January 2016 I had a complete surprise when I was told by staff that I had been recalled back to my local hospital. That morning, I actually had an appointment at a Cancer Centre in Central London to check the lumps in my breast. The appointment was put on hold and I was later transferred to a local psychiatric hospital instead. When I arrived there, I was not given a room; I was told that I would have to see a doctor to be assessed. I waited seven hours before I was seen and was surprised when my care co-ordinator showed up with the ward doctor to see me. After a lengthy conversation I was surprised when I was told that I could be discharged on a Community Treatment Order (CTO). A CTO is an order that has been made which means that I have to stick to certain conditions whilst I am in the community, or my doctor could possibly recall me back to hospital. The conditions that I had to abide with included taking all prescribed medication including depot injections. I also had to see the mental health team regularly. My section 3 was due to run out the following day. When I left the hospital, I took a cab to my parent's house, though later decided to go to my own flat. I had been missing my flat very much and just wanted to be there. My flat was in a complete mess. I had been decorating before I went into hospital and everything was still all over the place. Initially the heating and hot water was not working and it was very cold in the flat, though they both came on later that evening. I managed to get myself something to eat and then I went to bed at around 1am.

It felt slightly strange being in the flat by myself, after having been around people 24/7 for the past year. I was saddened when only a day after coming out of hospital, by the following evening I became unwell again. I called my mother and after telling her that I was not well, she rushed to come and see me. I felt very depressed and was also feeling suicidal, I just could not cope. I decided to call an ambulance and was taken to a local general hospital. The following day I was taken back to where I was before because there were no beds in Islington. The next day, I had time to sleep and reflect on things. I felt that things had not worked out for me when I had been discharged because I had been kept in hospital for so long. I had been in hospital for six months and had only been out by myself a few times. I did not think it would be so difficult coming out of hospital but it was. I needed a better transition back into the community. I had been asking for home leave, but had only been back to my flat twice. Coming out of hospital felt very strange to me.

While I was a patient in hospital I wrote many letters to various different people and organisations including a letter to the manager of the hospital and the head office of the hospital. I had been suffering for so many years and so many people and organisations had been deliberately treating me so unfairly. I had been crying out for help for years, though it seemed that the only one who was willing to help me was the Almighty God. I was not in contact with any Christians while I was in hospital apart from some of the staff who claimed to be Christians, though were part of a system treating me badly. On the 2nd February 2016, it was my birthday and I was still in hospital. In the morning I was allowed to go out on leave by myself, I enjoyed this. When I arrived back on the ward some members of staff decided to provoke me which resulted in me getting angry. Eventually staff offered me PRN medication; I decided to take the tablets instead of having an injection. I was very disappointed that I was treated so badly on my birthday.

Something important that I was trying my best to control was my anger. When I was a patient at one hospital, I had actually asked staff if any anger management sessions were available because I knew that I was beginning to have difficulties in this area. I was told that I could have the sessions, but I decided not to have it because it would have been with a psychologist whom I had problems with when she worked with me at another hospital. I found it very frustrating while I was a patient. I am not usually an aggressive person, though I was really fed up of people inflicting so much physical pain on me for no apparent reason, so I decided to attack back. I informed staff that when I get angry, that it would help if they still treated me with respect. I do not feel that offering me medication helps or forcing injections on me. This just makes me angrier. I do not think that provocation, ridicule, assault, harassment, discrimination or abuse helps, yet this is what I was having to put up with in the hospital. I usually have a few mixed feelings about the issue of psychology, though while I was in hospital, I had quite a few psychology sessions with a male psychologist which I found helpful. I also enjoyed doing regular art therapy sessions. It was very nice to have the opportunity to get off of the ward, which was often chaotic and noisy.

Something that I found very difficult to understand was that when staff in the hospitals did something wrong, nothing would happen to them. But when I did something wrong I was quickly injected and my leave was suspended. The hospitals, especially my current one were committing serious crimes against me and seemed to be getting away with it. I had reported these crimes to the police in the past, though nothing had been done to help me. Being a Christian, I know that the God whom I serve will never let me down and I will receive full justice one day. I noticed that I was being treated very differently to the other patients. I saw some of the patients at the hospital initially do worse things than me and they were never offered PRN, or taken to the de-escalation room to be injected. When I was attacked by another patient, I did not see staff offer her any medication and she was not taken to the de-escalation room. I can only imagine that if I had attacked a white patient, the same way that I was attacked by a white woman, then I would have been in serious trouble because I am a black woman. When I was first injected I had never touched or attacked anybody. I do feel that the negative way that I am often treated partly because I am a black woman. I feel that if I were white, then I would not go through so many difficulties. However, I have actually been treated very badly by many black people too. If I think about things carefully, I have been treated badly by people from all different nationalities.

I was shocked when a male staff member injected me in the lower back and not even my bottom once. There were two other men present in the room at the time. About two weeks later, I began to develop terrible pains in my lower back, which I felt in and being treated unfairly. There is a scripture in the Bible that I am aware of in Matthew:10.28-29- 'And do not fear those who kill the body but cannot kill the soul. But rather fear Him who is able to destroy both soul and body in hell'.

Something that I thought deeply about while I was at hospital was that some of the staff there and in other hospitals liked to tell me that they had children. Some of these same staff were individuals who would often treat me in a negative way by disrespecting me. I often wondered what type of example they were setting for their children to follow and what type of role models they were. I thought that some of their children may ask their parents, 'What did you do at work today mummy?' Or 'What did you do at work today daddy?' Would their parents tell their children the truth, like they deliberately treated a patient disrespectfully at work today, or would they lie to them? Would they tell them about the woman who was injected over forty times at their work place? Will they tell their children that mummy or daddy work in a place where a woman was physically attacked by another patient and is now in pain every day and that the hospital and the police have done nothing about it? Will these parents teach their children the importance of treating people in a fair and caring way? Will they teach their children the importance of justice? Then will those same parents still come to work and treat me badly? It really makes me wonder what type of parents these people are. I actually think that they are bad parents; then again I am not a parent myself at the moment.

Whenever I go to hospital, sometimes I have issues with the food which is not always such a bad thing because it usually encourages me too fast.

Whilst at hospital I had difficulties eating there sometimes. I only ate vegan and vegetarian food while I was at the hospital. I actually think that sometimes I was frustrated because I was not eating properly. Being a qualified and experienced chef who has a diploma in nutrition, I appreciate good, healthy, well cooked food. There was one time when I developed food poisoning whilst being a patient in hospital. I was surprised that when I rushed to vomit in the toilet, one of the staff came and asked me if I wanted her to massage my back. I felt that this was highly insensitive. On two other occasions I found strange things in my food. One was a piece of paper, though staff told me that it was potato skin. I told them that I was a writer and a chef and knew the difference between potato skin and paper. On another occasion, I saw what looked like a piece of meat in my vegan food. The staff did not take me seriously including the chef who I asked to see but did not come and see me. There was one time when I ordered a cheese and tomato baguette and found corned beef on the outside. I felt that even the catering department were deliberately tampering with my food. When I told the doctor that I once had food poisoning and that I vomited he told me that I was paranoid. After a series of strange things happening with my food I decided to stop eating and even stopped drinking water for seven weeks in the hospital. I began to buy food from outside when I was allowed out on leave. I also did some dry fasting which I was very pleased about.

There were many times when I went to bed feeling very hungry while I was at hospital. This was when I was not eating the hospital food and I was not allowed out on leave. I was concerned that I was actually putting on weight I think that this was because the dose of the medication had been increased and I was not eating the correct foods. I was tending to buy a lot of snacks when I went to the shops such as crisps and sweets which were unhealthy. In the space of a couple of months I had put on a stone and a half. In the Bible, it states that we should not worry about what we will eat or drink. I was struggling to eat in hospital, especially at night when I would often be hungry. I would think about how I would get food the following day, but God would always provide for me.

On the 14th April 2016, I received a letter from the hospital manager. I had actually written a letter to him a couple of weeks upon my arrival at the hospital after I was attacked by another patient and I felt that I was being treated unfairly by staff. I had requested to see the manager and was told that he would come and see me on a particular day within an hour, though he never showed up. The letter that I received from the hospital manager was in response to a letter which I had sent to the head office. I was very disappointed that nobody from the head office got in contact with me, instead an investigation into my complaint was carried out internally which I was not satisfied with. Eventually I told the ward staff that I wanted to meet the manager and I was able too. When I spoke to the manager, the two main issues that I brought to his attention was the fact that another patient had been allowed to so easily attack me resulting in me being left with an injury and nothing had been done about it. Also I told the hospital manager that I had been given over forty injections in my bottom and felt that I was being treated unfairly. I was shocked when the manager informed me that there was no evidence that I was attacked. When I told him that there were CCTV cameras all over the hospital, he then informed me that the hospital only keeps footage for a certain amount of time. Regarding all the injections that I had at the hospital, the manager said that injections were only given to me when they were necessary. I found it very sad that a black man in his position could knowingly allow me to suffer in his hospital the way in which I had been. I began to think that maybe he had a wife or other female relatives like me and I was sure that he would not want them to go through what I was going through, but he did nothing to help me. On one of the wards that I stayed on at this hospital, I noticed racist graffiti written in the toilets I informed staff though did not seem very concerned.

I had been at this particular hospital for nine months and it was very frustrating especially as my doctor in the hospital had been telling me that I did not need to be there. I was being kept there against my will and I felt that psychological experiments were being done on me. One afternoon my primary nurse said that she wanted to talk to me. I was quite surprised when she told me that I had been recalled back to my local hospital, a bed had become available. I stayed at my local hospital until July 2016; I was allowed to go on extended leave until I was finally discharged and placed on a Community Treatment Order. Before I was discharged, I still had to go back to the hospital every month for depot injections. I was very saddened when the hospital doctor increased the dose of the medication that I was on. The medication had been increased five times this year and it was giving me terrible side effects.

Something else that happened before I was discharged was that a new community mental health team in Islington was assigned to me. I was happy that I would no longer have to work with my old team. However, it still concerned me that I still had to work with a team in Islington. I am fed up with mental health teams interfering in my life causing me to be unhappy and I would love to be left alone. I think that somebody needs to take responsibility for all the negative things that health services have done to me and needs to be held accountable. I think that it is a total disgrace that mental health services in London have caused me so much distress and nobody seems to be acknowledging how or why I get sick in the first place.

I think that it is a miracle that I am still alive. The fact that I have many people who have and continue to harm me makes me realise that I have a lot of enemies. Though it also makes me realise that I am a very special woman, if so many people are being so wicked towards me for no reason. I have to admit that I have done some things wrong in the past and I may have offended people. Since I became a Christian, I understand the importance of treating people with love and respect. I do actually believe in the saying, 'What goes around comes around', in other words if you treat some one bad eventually something bad will happen to you. Maybe I am paying the price for some of the things that I have done wrong in the past. Though every day, I repent of my sins and ask for God's forgiveness. If I offend someone I usually try to apologise to them when I realise that I have done wrong.

In January 2016, after having only spent six months in the community, I ended up back in hospital again. As I am adding the finishing touches to my manuscript for this book, it is currently the 28th July 2017. I was placed on a section 3 and have been a patient in hospital now for just over six months. Different doctors have continued to try me on different medications which still give me side effects. Another difficult event that recently took place in my life was to hear the very sad news that my dad had died, while I was in hospital. My dad had been ill for a long time, so I pray that he is now resting in peace. After I heard the news about my father, I was so upset and angry that I ripped up and placed in the bin some of my writing that I had done, for three months whilst being in hospital. I even decided that I did not want to finish writing and publishing this book. After careful thought and consideration and the way my dad used to encourage me to write as a child, I have decided to finish this book and get it published as soon as possible.

Chapter 3

Power To The People

POWER TO THE PEOPLE

Power can be defined as strength, control, energy, authority or the ability to do something. Power can come from many different sources for example, the government, police force, army, monarchy, even electricity etc. Being a Born Again Christian, I have come to the realisation that all power ultimately comes from an Omnipotent Almighty God. He then gives us power and the ability to do things. I believe in the Trinity which includes God the Father, God the Son and God the Holy Spirit-three in one. By having a personal relationship with God through Jesus Christ, it is possible for us humans to be filled with Gods Holy Spirit which gives us power.

So what does Gods power (The Holy Spirit) give us the ability to do? According to scripture, the Bible states that I can do all things Through Christ who strengthens me Philippians 4:13. There has been times in my life when I felt that I was incapable of doing certain things, however when I eventually place my faith in God, He helps me to believe in myself and the Holy Spirit then enables me to do the very thing which I felt that I could not do. Without faith, it is impossible to please God. Prayer is an important way to please God and grow spiritually. By praying, we build up our relationship with God and we are able to ask Him for want we want in Jesus name and receive it, providing that it is something that will benefit us.

Jesus Christ was persecuted and crucified. His blood was shed so that we could be saved and set free from sin and death. There is power in the blood of Jesus Christ. Without the shedding of Christ's blood, there would be no free gift of salvation available to us. Jesus had plenty of Holy Ghost Power. He was able to perform miracles. Eventually when He was crucified and died, He managed to rise and live again. I believe in miracles, not just because I have read about them in the Bible, but because I have actually experienced some. I have evidence that Jesus is alive, although I cannot see Him: He has done many things for me. I am now in a position where I want to spread the good news to let others know that we can receive power from God and do what we thought was impossible. The Bible mentions that we shall receive power-: Acts:1-8 'But you shall receive power when the Holy Spirit has come upon you; and you shall be witnesses to Me in Jerusalem, and in all Judea and Samaria, and to the end of the earth'.

I have a strong desire to be an evangelist, I am in the process of getting my training and teaching from my Head Master- Jesus Christ. I believe that we are now living in the end times, there is so much pain and suffering that exists with famines, disease, wars etc. I do not believe that God causes pain or suffering, though I do believe that He has the power to take it away. I believe in the second coming of Jesus and that one day there will be Heaven and peace on earth. In the meantime, we have to live in this world which at times can be extremely difficult, but with Jesus we can be more than conquerors and have the ability to overcome. I think that it is amazing to be able to have part of Gods Holy Spirit inside of us, which makes us to be like Him, by certain characteristics and traits that we have. The Bible speaks of the fruit of the Spirit, which can be produced inside of a person when they have received the baptism of the Holy Spirit. This includes, love, joy, peace, longsuffering, kindness, goodness, faithfulness, gentleness, and self-control - Galatians 5:22-23. Many people often refer to love as being a very powerful thing. God himself is love and love never fails. There are also gifts of the Holy Spirit, which includes -: wisdom, knowledge, the gift of healing, the working of miracles, prophesy, discerning of spirits, different kinds of tongues and the interpretation of tongues-: 1 Corinthians 12: 8-10

If we take the Christian viewpoint, as opposed to the Big Bang Theory/ The Theory of Evolution and The origin of Species by Charles Darwin. According to the Holy Bible, we can see that in the beginning, God created the heavens and the earth-: Genesis 1:1 God also created humans and all living creatures. The creation of the world must be one of the most powerful things that has taken place as well as the resurrection of Jesus Christ. These days, there is much emphasis placed on what makes a person powerful and it usually has something to do with how much material wealth they have. There is nothing wrong with having material things; though God calls us to seek first the kingdom of God and His righteousness. So how does a person receive Gods Holy Spirit? In my case, I first became saved. To be saved in the Christian context means that a person accepts Jesus Christ as their Lord and personal saviour. Salvation is a free gift from Jesus and it is by Gods amazing grace that we are saved. Over a period of time, after becoming saved I then began to change by praying and reading my Bible. I became a Christian in the year 2000 and I am now able to speak in tongues, which is evidence that I am filled with the Holy Spirit. Speaking in tongues is when a person speaks in a spiritual language with their mouth which God understands. It is a powerful thing and a great gift to have. However, I know that I am not perfect, not yet; though I believe that one day I will be, by the time I get to Heaven, I will be just like Jesus.

The Bible states that if we call upon the name of the Lord, we shall be saved. It also says, Ask and you shall receive, seek and you shall find, knock and the door shall be open. The baptism of the Holy Spirit is when a person is filled with Gods Spirit; there is also a term which is known as the baptism of fire that refers to a fiery trial of faith where suffering takes place in order to purify the faithful. When I look at and evaluate my own life since becoming a Christian, I have to admit and say that I have faced many more difficult challenges since I became saved, but I am now much stronger than I was before and better able to deal with difficulties that life often brings. Though it has to be said, I still do make mistakes, I am human though God is very forgiving and merciful. The issue of forgiveness leads me on to talk about the importance of repentance. Repentance is when an individual feels and expresses remorse or regrets something that they have done. If we do something wrong or commit a sin, it is always a good idea if we can go to God and ask for His forgiveness. From my experience, if I do something wrong and I do not acknowledge to myself and to God about what I have done, the guilt, shame and disgrace usually starts to affect me like some kind of disease. It may seem as though there are many things that we need to do and consider in order to receive power from God, yes this is true. The Bible states that faith without works is dead - James 2:26. I think that any good thing that we want in life usually requires us to make some form of sacrifice for us to achieve it. It makes it feel that much sweeter when we get what we have been after because we have had to work and put some effort into it.

Jesus Christ paid the ultimate sacrifice for us when He died on the cross. God allowed His only son to go through severe pain and suffering so that we could be redeemed. Though He did it because of His love for us-: 'For God so loved the world that He gave His only begotten Son, that whoever should believe in Him should not perish but have eternal life'-: John 3:16.

I have heard that when a person has too much power, it can be a bad thing. I would agree with this statement because too much of anything is in excess. As mentioned above, one of the fruits of the Spirit is self-control. Along with wisdom and knowledge, it is imperative that Christians use the power that they have been given wisely, although the Holy Spirit should help them to do this. Quite often, in today's society we hear of certain individuals who have abused their position of authority and misused the power which they have been given. It is even possible for Christians to abuse the power that they have been given if it is not used correctly. Personally, I feel that I should try to set a good example for others to follow if I want to help lead people to Christ. The Devil (Satan) who was originally called Lucifer was an important angel in heaven, but because he abused his position of power by wanting to be God, God cast him out of heaven. It was the devil, in the form of a serpent that tempted Adam and Eve in the Garden of Eden. They both chose to disobey God and that was when sin came into the world. The world that we now live in contains evil and I believe that the devil is the cause of this. However, because of Jesus Christ, we still have hope. I know that when I disobey God, from experience I usually have problems. According to Bible scripture, God will never leave us or forsake us, but if we have sin in our lives it puts a distance between us and God, then eventually we lose the authority that He has given us. God loves everybody, even people who do not believe or do not follow Him. Though when we do choose to believe and follow Him, we are able to benefit more from what He has to offer which includes blessings, an abundant life and eventually eternal life. We still face difficulties and challenges even if we believe in God, though I feel that it will all be worth it in the end when Jesus returns one day and takes His chosen ones to Heaven. I do believe that there is a hell and when Jesus returns to judge all of us, some people will go there. I hope and pray that I am not one of them.

Another name for God in Hebrew is Jehovah, Jehovah Jireh means that the Lord will provide. God has given us His word in the form of the Holy Bible that contains important scriptures regarding how we should live our lives. The first and greatest commandment is that we should love the lord our God with all our heart, soul and strength- Mark 12:30. In the Bible, there were many powerful men and women of God who faced difficulties but were able to overcome with Gods help, such as Moses, Abraham, Joshua, Ruth, Samuel, Esther and Job etc. Job suffered severe hardship and a great loss in his life, but because of his faithfulness to God, he eventually gained a great deal of prosperity. Samuel was a prophet, judge and a priest. Esther was a queen and Ruth was a woman who showed great love, humility and respect to others.

In my opening paragraph, I mentioned the army as an example of having power. God has an army which is made up of Christian soldiers. Life can be a constant battle sometimes, especially as the devil came to steal kill and destroy. The devil is often referred to as the prince of darkness and Jesus is known as the prince of peace. The devil is out to ruin people's lives and at times does so, but God is able to equip and empower us. Christian soldiers have a spiritual battle to fight, not a physical one. God tells us to put on the whole armour of God, a Christian soldiers uniform. This includes the sword of the Spirit which is the word of God so that we can fight against evil. When we confess God's word with our mouths and quote scripture, this is very powerful, for the word of God is living and powerful and sharper than any two edged sword - Hebrews 4:16. The Holy Bible is no ordinary book, yes some books can transform a person's life, I have heard of this. However, if read and used correctly the Bible can help to save, heal, prosper, protect, provide for, nourish, strengthen, comfort, deliver and encourage, as well as many other things. I have not yet read the whole of the Bible, however when I read certain scriptures, I find that it is a great source of encouragement and inspiration to me How we live our lives now will eventually determine how we will live in the future. Becoming a Born Again Christian, was the best decision that I have ever made and will ever make. I have been baptised in water, which is something that God requires every new believer to do. The full immersion into water represents the individual moving from an old life into a new one. Nowadays, there are many different religions and different faiths. The Bible says that there is only one way to God and that is through Jesus Christ. I remember the day when I became saved, it was amazing and powerful. It felt as though God had taken away the heavy burden I had been carrying for so long, which included anger, bitterness, resentment, confusion, low self-esteem and un-forgiveness. For the first time in my life I began to understand what my life meant. Over a period of time, God has given me various gifts, I believe that we are all gifted in some type of way; we just need time to discover what that gift is and nurture it in order for it to grow and develop.

In order to conclude this topic regarding power, I pray that God will pour out His Holy Spirit and that His light will shine upon us all, now and forever more.

HOLY GHOST POWER TO THE PEOPLE!

Chapter 4

Led By The Holy Spirit

LED BY THE HOLY SPIRIT

Since I became a Christian, I have been praying almost every day to God, for him to guide and direct me. God is perfect and He has great and wonderful plans for us. When we are filled with the Holy Spirit we have a deeper connection and relationship with God. When we are led by the Holy Spirit, we are more likely to do what God wants us to do. It is a real pleasure to know Jesus and I am so glad that I became a Christian. I am happy to say that I believe I have been filled with some of God's Holy Spirit, otherwise I do not think that I would have confidently been able to write this book.

It is possible to become like Christ by having particular characteristics that come though the infilling and Baptism of the Holy Spirit. To be able to have a 'Christ Like Character,' can only be a good thing because God is good all the time. God the Father, Son and Spirit are all one (The Trinity) I often pray to God, for Him to give me qualities and characteristics like Him, I want to be just like Jesus.

Sometimes in life, we may come across barriers which try to prevent us from moving forward in life and achieving what we want to achieve. A barrier could be said to be an obstacle that prevents you from getting to a certain place. Barriers can come in all different ways. it could be something physical or spiritual. I have experienced different barriers in my life many times. This has included such things as discrimination and harassment. God has taught me that there is a way that we can break through the Barriers and obtain success and victory. As I am currently writing this book, it is 04.35am on the 30th July 2017. I am in a psychiatric department at the moment and I have been in hospital, on this admission for over six months. Despite the many difficulties that I have and continue to experience in my life, I would like testify and declare that I have victory and I am not a looser, but a winner. I do not consider my life to be a sad one. I have had many sad moments in my life, however I have had many happy ones too. I have faith to believe that my life will improve.

I consider the devil to be a looser because he has very evil and wicked intentions. He wants to destroy people's lives and cause distress, misery and suffering. Jesus Christ was crucified and died so that we can be saved from sin and death. The battle is already won, because Jesus conquered and rose from the grave and now He lives and reigns. As I have mentioned earlier in this book, even Christians suffer and go through difficulties sometimes. Right now I am having physical pains in my body. Some of this pain has been caused by side effects of medication that doctors have been forcing me to take. Also some of the pain has been caused by being physically attacked by people in the past. Also I have had quite a few accidents where for some strange reason I have banged my head on fourteen different occasions. I have had pain in my body almost every day for over three years now. Although I go through a lot of suffering and pain, I also sometimes experience immense joy and satisfaction. I will be honest and say that it can be difficult to be happy when you are in pain for so long. I do feel sad sometimes, even depressed on occasions. Believing in Jesus Christ gives me hope and He also helps me to believe in myself. Jesus has the power to heal the sick and perform miracles, but He does it in His own time. I have heard that people can be healed instantly by Jesus. I have also heard that some people suffer for a long time, even when they have a strong faith. Some Christians even die from sickness.

Death has always been a mystery to me. My father recently died after having been ill for a long time. I know that he believed in God, but as far as I know, he was not a Christian or saved. I have recently been thinking if my father will eventually get to Heaven. The last time that I saw my father, I remember him smiling at me, but I knew he was very sick. I never thought to myself that it would be the last time that I would see him again. I have since seen my father in a dream that I recently had. In the dream, my whole family was there at a party. My father was sitting on a chair and I went up to him and we hugged each other. I am currently a patient in a psychiatric hospital which happens to be very close to a large cemetery. When I look out of the bedroom window, I can see a couple of tomb stones in the distance. Tomb stones and cemeteries used to frighten me, but not anymore. In a couple of weeks' time, most of my family in London will be travelling to Ghana for my dad's funeral. I will not be attending.

It is my intention to come out of hospital as soon as possible and be more independent. I do not consider myself to be mentally ill at the moment, so I should not be a patient in a psychiatric hospital. I look forward to my future and I will get ready for the amazing things that God has in store for me. Some years ago some particular words came to my mind. The words were 'Never underestimate the power of God.' I believe that this was a word from God. God has spoken to me many times, in different ways. God speaks to me mainly through His word in scriptures that I read in the Holy Bible. God has also spoken directly to me in the past in the form of an inner voice. The voice of God gives hope and is very positive, unlike the voice of the devil which is dangerous and harmful. I expect the unexpected when it comes to God, because He has a way of surprising me when He is ready, not when I am ready. God's surprises are always wonderful and His timing is perfect.

My biggest dream is for me to be able to make a positive difference in the world. I believe that God will help me to achieve this.

Poems

I AM NOBODY'S SLAVE

I am nobody's slave
And I don't wear no chains
But this mental health system
Has turned me into a victim
A victim to prescribed poison, discrimination is the reason
The doctors call it medicine
I call it a toxic body damaging weapon

I am nobody's slave
And I don't wear no chains
But the wickedness and the hate
Is just too much for me to take and tolerate
The pain that I have been through often brings me to tears
At times I know not what to do
And that's sometimes one of my fears.

I've been held down by men
Even though I'm a woman
I've had my pants pulled down
And injected in the bum,
Even though I was restrained and couldn't run
The humiliation and the degradation
is more than just imagination

I am nobody's slave
And I don't wear no chains
I've been sedated and assaulted, I've not been whipped
And I am nobody's nigger
But these are serious crimes,
To be injected almost 300 times in the bum
Though nobody used a gun and pulled a trigger

The side effects from the drugs
And the disrespect
is far too much for me to take
Please, for goodness sake
How much more do you think I can take?
You are not real health professionals
You are all fake.

I am nobody's slave
And I don't wear no chains
The torture and the torment made me want to end my life
The stress and the pressure
Made it hard for me to want to stay alive
They've got me locked up right now as I am writing
Then they wonder why at times I get angry and start fighting

You may kill my body but not my soul
You may think that you are winning
But you will never be in control
I was born black for a reason,
Because my colour is a beautiful shade
Though God knew that I would face racism and discrimination
That's why He also made me bold and brave

I am nobody's slave
And I don't wear no chains
No chains do I wear so why do you dare
To do what you do
You are being so cruel
With your torture you ought to just leave me alone
Your wickedness almost cuts through to my bones

Though I will not worry
Because I know that I am free
You will be ashamed and disgraced, just wait and see
I will stay strong
I know it's you bad people that are doing wrong
I know that I'm not perfect,
but what you are doing really isn't worth it

I am nobody's slave
and I don't wear no chains
Who the Son sets free is free indeed
I'm a Born Again Christian with some faith to believe that
God will protect and keep me brave and safe
I have faith to believe that no matter what you do
God will always do much better than you.

POOR PATIENT CARE

So you lock me up, and then drug me up
You feed me then almost physically beat me
You say that you care
Though your hospital treatment is not at all fair
You offer me coffee and cups of tea
Though I can see
That your poor patient care is destroying me

You inject me until I struggle to walk
You sedate me so that I cannot talk
You poison my food
Then when I complain
You make it seem as though I am being rude
Every day I feel pain
Though you ridicule me like this is just a game

You actually get paid
To treat me like this
When you get paid, I wonder what is on your shopping list
Do you go home at the end of your shift?
And ever think about how I feel?
Because I'm the one left with physical and emotional scars
I'm the one left feeling more ill

When you do wrong, nothing is said
If I say or do wrong, you harm me for so long
That I often get more sick and wish I were dead
You are actually supposed to help me to recover
Though you treat me so bad that I do not get better
Management do nothing to correct the situation
And the hospital offers me little protection.

THAT TIME OF THE MONTH

It's that time of the month again, the period thing
It doesn't bother me that much
I don't suffer with PMT
I'm still able to praise the Lord as per usual and sing.

I get through so many sanitary towels
Maybe I should get shares in the company
I get no stomach pain which is great
At times I feel stronger than on non-period days.

I have not started the menopause yet
So I am used to this.
I'm in no hurry to start
Because one day I just might want to have kids.

It's that time of the month again
When wearing white trousers or a white skirt
For me just isn't the done thing
If you know what I mean!

It's that bloody time of the month again
When I am reminded that I am a woman
Men don't have to go through this
Though I love being a woman, it's something
I would not want to miss.

BEAUTIFUL WOMAN

Am I a beautiful woman?
I have dark brown skin with a big nose and big lips
I have short hair, big thighs and large hips.

Am I a beautiful woman?
I have a big belly and I'm a couple of stone overweight
Is that why I rarely get asked out by men to go out for a date?

Am I a beautiful woman?
I do not have model looks and I don't think that I could ever
Get on the front page of vogue magazine or beauty books.

Am I a beautiful woman?
I don't look as good as I used to when I was young
Since this maturity thing begun

Am I a beautiful woman?
I think to myself, yes indeed
Just believe.

Am I a beautiful woman?
I have beauty from within, I'm one of God's creations
Although I have dark skin.

WHAT HAS HAPPENED TO THE CHURCH?

What has happened to the church?
When I go there to pray
But pastors call the police on me
And I'm turned away.

What has happened to the church?
When they teach and preach the wrong thing
But Bishops and Pastors still insist
That we give tithes and offerings

What has happened to the church?
When they don't make me feel welcome
And they do what they can to drive me away
Because they don't want me to stay

What has happened to the church?
when they sing their fancy gospel and Christian songs
Though they discriminate and make me feel as though
I do not belong

What has happened to the church?
When I overhear pastors say that I am mad
Where is their love, compassion and understanding?
How can so called Christians treat me so bad?

What has happened to the church?
When pastors lay their hands on my head
They spin me around in circles
Telling me lies, such as a demon wants me dead

What has happened to the church?
People don't show much love anymore
Where have all the real Christians gone?
It's no surprise that many people won't go near a church door

What has happened to the church?
Some so called Christians have wicked and bad intentions
They gossip, tell lies and are jealous of others
They don't really care about fellow sisters and brothers.

What has happened to the church?

SEDATED FOR SEVENTEEN YEARS

A group called the Sounds of Blackness once sang a song
And some of the words were that
A genius has been asleep for too long

I think that genius used to be me
Because doctors are giving me different medications
and they are heavily sedating me

For years I have struggled to get up in the morning and
Sleeping to much really was a problem
The difficulties have been going on for so long

There have been times when I have felt physically
Weak and not strong
I could not function to the best of my ability

I struggled to be the beautiful woman
That I wanted to be
They deliberately abused me, it's now obvious to see

However, my life is not a sad story
It is actually a victorious one
Because I have faith in Jesus Christ, He's enabled me to overcome.

DEAR DAD

You have left us now dad and it hasn't been long
I miss you so much and I'm trying to be strong
Your smiling face and your warm embrace
Not forgetting your generosity and great hospitality

Your intelligence was outstanding
You taught me many things when I was a child
As I became an adult, you still continued to teach
You made me believe in myself and the future goals that I could reach

Before you left this world, you suffered so much
So now I hope that your soul is at peace
Even though your body will rest in the dust
although you have gone I will still sing songs

But I have unanswered questions and things I wanted to know
There are things about the past I wanted to learn about
As I continue to get older and grow
God is now my teacher and I loved the fact that you were a believer

You were not perfect, but then neither am I
You did some wrongs and made mistakes, though you also tried
Now I even miss your strange habits that used to get on my nerves
The world just isn't the same without you, men like you are few

REST IN PEACE DAD!

FORGIVENESS

Lord, help me to forgive
Help me to live in this world
Where so many people go out of their way to hurt me
Some of them don't see my pain
There are others that see, but feel no shame.

Lord, help me to forgive
Help me to love my enemies
They are many and I am one
Some try to be funny
But this wicked game is no fun

Lord, help me to forgive
Help me to understand that two wrongs
Do not make a right
So I must not seek revenge
Physically attack or fight

Lord, help me to forgive
My enemies conspire against me
Their evil wicked schemes are not so called 'Paranoia'
It is also not just in my imagination, this is not simply in my dreams
The devil is behind it all, the dark destroyer

Lord, help me to forgive
Help me to be more like you
The Bible says that if we don't forgive others
Then you will not forgive us too
Please Lord, help me to forgive.

READERS, PLEASE NOTE THAT THIS IS NOT THE END
BUT THE BEGINNING OF SOMETHING WONDERFUL!